THIS PLANNER BELONGS TO

____

HOME ORGANISER

THANK YOU SO MUCH FOR YOUR PURCHASE, OUR VERY SMALL BUSINESS APPRECIATES EVERY SINGLE CUSTOMER WE GET.

WE REALLY HOPE THIS PLANNER HELPS TO MAKE YOUR LIFE EASIER AND MORE ORGANISED.

CHECK OUT OUR OTHER BOOKS BY SEARCHING OUR AUTHOR NAME "**HELPFUL HOME PLANNERS**"

PLANNER INFORMATION + FEATURES:

- Customisable to do checklists - Organise cleaning tasks by room or priority, organise your shopping list into sections such as frozen, fresh, toiletries etc. The choice is yours.

- Weekly meal planner (x6) - So you can plan the meals in advance, and get the required shopping in one visit. After the 6 weeks, you can randomise as you like.

- Monthly budget planner - Keep track of your expenses, income, appointments, monthly goals, etc.

DAILY CHECKLISTS

DATE:

Living Room

- [x] Hoover
- [x] Carpet Freshener
- [x] Change Wax Melts
- [x] Tidy Coffee Table
- [x] Clean Sofa
- [ ]
- [ ]
- [ ]

Olivia's Bedroom

- [x] Change Bedding
- [x] Put Toys Away
- [x] Hoover
- [ ] Polish
- [ ] Clean Blinds
- [ ] Put Dirty Washing On
- [ ]
- [ ]

Jack's Bedroom

- [x] Clean Blinds
- [x] Change Light Bulb
- [x] Put Away Clothes
- [ ]
- [ ]
- [ ]
- [ ]
- [ ]

Shopping

- [ ] Milk
- [ ] Eggs
- [ ] Chicken Breasts
- [ ] Cereal
- [ ] Tea Bags
- [ ] Bread
- [ ] Cheese
- [ ] Juice

WEEKLY MEAL PLANNER

BREAKFAST	LUNCH	DINNER

BREAKFAST	LUNCH	DINNER

BREAKFAST	LUNCH	DINNER

BREAKFAST	LUNCH	DINNER

BREAKFAST	LUNCH	DINNER

BREAKFAST	LUNCH	DINNER

BREAKFAST	LUNCH	DINNER

WEEKLY MEAL PLANNER

BREAKFAST	LUNCH	DINNER

BREAKFAST	LUNCH	DINNER

BREAKFAST	LUNCH	DINNER

BREAKFAST	LUNCH	DINNER

BREAKFAST	LUNCH	DINNER

BREAKFAST	LUNCH	DINNER

BREAKFAST	LUNCH	DINNER

WEEKLY MEAL PLANNER

BREAKFAST	LUNCH	DINNER

BREAKFAST	LUNCH	DINNER

BREAKFAST	LUNCH	DINNER

BREAKFAST	LUNCH	DINNER

BREAKFAST	LUNCH	DINNER

BREAKFAST	LUNCH	DINNER

BREAKFAST	LUNCH	DINNER

WEEKLY MEAL PLANNER

BREAKFAST	LUNCH	DINNER

BREAKFAST	LUNCH	DINNER

BREAKFAST	LUNCH	DINNER

BREAKFAST	LUNCH	DINNER

BREAKFAST	LUNCH	DINNER

BREAKFAST	LUNCH	DINNER

BREAKFAST	LUNCH	DINNER

WEEKLY MEAL PLANNER

BREAKFAST	LUNCH	DINNER

BREAKFAST	LUNCH	DINNER

BREAKFAST	LUNCH	DINNER

BREAKFAST	LUNCH	DINNER

BREAKFAST	LUNCH	DINNER

BREAKFAST	LUNCH	DINNER

BREAKFAST	LUNCH	DINNER

WEEKLY MEAL PLANNER

BREAKFAST	LUNCH	DINNER

BREAKFAST	LUNCH	DINNER

BREAKFAST	LUNCH	DINNER

BREAKFAST	LUNCH	DINNER

BREAKFAST	LUNCH	DINNER

BREAKFAST	LUNCH	DINNER

BREAKFAST	LUNCH	DINNER

DAILY CHECKLISTS

DATE:

DAILY CHECKLISTS

DATE:

DAILY CHECKLISTS

DATE:

DAILY CHECKLISTS

DATE:

DAILY CHECKLISTS

DATE:

DAILY CHECKLISTS

DATE:

DAILY CHECKLISTS

DATE:

DAILY CHECKLISTS

DATE:

DAILY CHECKLISTS

DATE:

DAILY CHECKLISTS

DATE:

DAILY CHECKLISTS

DATE:

DAILY CHECKLISTS

DATE:

DAILY CHECKLISTS

DATE:

DAILY CHECKLISTS

DATE:

DAILY CHECKLISTS

DATE:

DAILY CHECKLISTS

DATE:

DAILY CHECKLISTS

DATE:

DAILY CHECKLISTS

DATE:

DAILY CHECKLISTS

DATE:

DAILY CHECKLISTS

DATE:

DAILY CHECKLISTS

DATE:

DAILY CHECKLISTS

DATE:

DAILY CHECKLISTS

DATE:

DAILY CHECKLISTS

DATE:

DAILY CHECKLISTS

DATE:

DAILY CHECKLISTS

DATE:

DAILY CHECKLISTS

DATE:

DAILY CHECKLISTS

DATE:

DAILY CHECKLISTS

DATE:

DAILY CHECKLISTS

DATE:

DAILY CHECKLISTS

DATE:

DAILY CHECKLISTS

DATE:

DAILY CHECKLISTS

DATE:

DAILY CHECKLISTS

DATE:

DAILY CHECKLISTS

DATE:

DAILY CHECKLISTS

DATE:

DAILY CHECKLISTS

DATE:

DAILY CHECKLISTS

DATE:

DAILY CHECKLISTS

DATE:

DAILY CHECKLISTS

DATE:

DAILY CHECKLISTS

DATE:

DAILY CHECKLISTS

DATE:

DAILY CHECKLISTS

DATE:

DAILY CHECKLISTS

DATE:

DAILY CHECKLISTS

DATE:

DAILY CHECKLISTS

DATE:

DAILY CHECKLISTS

DATE:

DAILY CHECKLISTS

DATE:

DAILY CHECKLISTS

DATE:

DAILY CHECKLISTS

DATE:

DAILY CHECKLISTS

DATE:

DAILY CHECKLISTS

DATE:

DAILY CHECKLISTS

DATE:

DAILY CHECKLISTS

DATE:

DAILY CHECKLISTS

DATE:

DAILY CHECKLISTS

DATE:

DAILY CHECKLISTS

DATE:

DAILY CHECKLISTS

DATE:

DAILY CHECKLISTS

DATE:

DAILY CHECKLISTS

DATE:

DAILY CHECKLISTS

DATE:

DAILY CHECKLISTS

DATE:

DAILY CHECKLISTS

DATE:

DAILY CHECKLISTS

DATE:

DAILY CHECKLISTS

DATE:

DAILY CHECKLISTS

DATE:

DAILY CHECKLISTS

DATE:

DAILY CHECKLISTS

DATE:

DAILY CHECKLISTS

DATE:

DAILY CHECKLISTS

DATE:

DAILY CHECKLISTS

DATE:

DAILY CHECKLISTS

DATE:

DAILY CHECKLISTS

DATE:

DAILY CHECKLISTS

DATE:

DAILY CHECKLISTS

DATE:

DAILY CHECKLISTS

DATE:

DAILY CHECKLISTS

DATE:

DAILY CHECKLISTS

DATE:

DAILY CHECKLISTS

DATE:

DAILY CHECKLISTS

DATE:

DAILY CHECKLISTS

DATE:

DAILY CHECKLISTS

DATE:

DAILY CHECKLISTS

DATE:

DAILY CHECKLISTS

DATE:

DAILY CHECKLISTS

DATE:

DAILY CHECKLISTS

DATE:

DAILY CHECKLISTS

DATE:

DAILY CHECKLISTS

DATE:

FINANCES

MONTH:

EXPENSE	AMOUNT	PAID
TOTAL		

INCOME

MONTH:

INCOME	AMOUNT	PAID
TOTAL		

NOTES

GOALS:

BIRTHDAYS:

FINANCES

MONTH:

EXPENSE	AMOUNT	PAID
TOTAL		

INCOME

MONTH:

INCOME	AMOUNT	PAID
TOTAL		

NOTES

GOALS:

BIRTHDAYS:

FINANCES

MONTH:

EXPENSE	AMOUNT	PAID
TOTAL		

INCOME

MONTH:

INCOME	AMOUNT	PAID
TOTAL		

NOTES

GOALS:

BIRTHDAYS:

FINANCES

MONTH:

EXPENSE	AMOUNT	PAID
TOTAL		

INCOME

MONTH:

INCOME	AMOUNT	PAID
TOTAL		

NOTES

GOALS:

BIRTHDAYS:

FINANCES

MONTH:

EXPENSE	AMOUNT	PAID
TOTAL		

INCOME

MONTH:

INCOME	AMOUNT	PAID
TOTAL		

NOTES

GOALS:

BIRTHDAYS:

FINANCES

MONTH:

EXPENSE	AMOUNT	PAID
TOTAL		

INCOME

MONTH:

INCOME	AMOUNT	PAID
TOTAL		

NOTES

GOALS:

BIRTHDAYS:

FINANCES

MONTH:

EXPENSE	AMOUNT	PAID
TOTAL		

INCOME

MONTH:

INCOME	AMOUNT	PAID
TOTAL		

NOTES

GOALS:

BIRTHDAYS:

FINANCES

MONTH:

EXPENSE	AMOUNT	PAID
TOTAL		

INCOME

MONTH:

INCOME	AMOUNT	PAID
TOTAL		

NOTES

GOALS:

BIRTHDAYS:

FINANCES

MONTH:

EXPENSE	AMOUNT	PAID
TOTAL		

INCOME

MONTH:

INCOME	AMOUNT	PAID
TOTAL		

NOTES

GOALS:

BIRTHDAYS:

FINANCES

MONTH:

EXPENSE	AMOUNT	PAID
TOTAL		

INCOME

MONTH:

INCOME	AMOUNT	PAID
TOTAL		

NOTES

GOALS:

BIRTHDAYS:

FINANCES

MONTH:

EXPENSE	AMOUNT	PAID
TOTAL		

INCOME

MONTH:

INCOME	AMOUNT	PAID
TOTAL		

NOTES

GOALS:

BIRTHDAYS:

FINANCES

MONTH:

EXPENSE	AMOUNT	PAID
TOTAL		

INCOME

MONTH:

INCOME	AMOUNT	PAID
TOTAL		

NOTES

GOALS:

BIRTHDAYS:

Printed in Great Britain
by Amazon